better together*

*This book is best read together, grownup and kid.

 akidsco.com

a
kids
book
about

a kids book about Judaism

יהדות

by M.M. Friedman

a kids book about

Text and design copyright © 2023
by A Kids Book About, Inc.

Copyright is good! It ensures that work like this can exist, and more work in the future can be created.

All rights reserved. No part of this publication may be reproduced, distributed, or transmitted in any form or by any means, including photocopying, recording, other electronic or mechanical methods, without the prior written permission of the publisher, except in the case of brief quotations embodied in critical reviews and certain other noncommercial uses permitted by copyright law. For permission requests, write to the publisher.

A Kids Book About, Kids Are Ready, and the colophon 'a' are trademarks of A Kids Book About, Inc.

Printed in the United States of America.

A Kids Book About books are available online: *akidsco.com*

To share your stories, ask questions, or inquire about bulk purchases (schools, libraries, and nonprofits), please use the following email address: *hello@akidsco.com*

Print ISBN: 978-1-958825-37-2
Ebook ISBN: 978-1-958825-38-9

Designed by Rick DeLucco
Edited by Emma Wolf

To every kid out there questioning,
learning, growing, and discovering
the world around them.

Intro

It isn't difficult to find information about Jewish people. A lot of both positive and negative information exists describing one of the smallest, but historically first, monotheistic religions out there. Where should parents turn to teach kids about the joys and beauty of Orthodox Judaism?

This book is here to give you a brief introduction and short overview about where the Jewish people originated, some of the laws and traditions still honored today, and how kindness, compassion, and being empathetic to others are all at the core of what it means to be Jewish.

This book is here for grownups and kids to learn more about Judaism, as well as to discover and be proud of their Jewish heritage.

Hi, my name is Menachem Friedman and I'm from Brooklyn, New York.

Almost everyone calls me Mendy—
I hope you will too.

This is a book about **Judaism**.

If I wrote a book that told you everything about Judaism, it might take a whole lifetime to read.

But we just don't have that much time!

So let's start with the basics...

What is Judaism?

Judaism is a religion.

Those who practice Judaism believe there is 1 God only and that this God provides a way of life that is fulfilling and kind.

We also believe God gave the **Torah** תּוֹרָה (toh-ruh) to the Jewish people.

The Torah is written in an ancient language still spoken today called Hebrew.

The Torah contains all the ways, rules, ethics, and traditions for us to live by, which are called **mitzvahs** מִצְווֹת (mitz-vahs).*

*There are 613 mitzvahs, to be exact.

I can't remember a time when Judaism wasn't essential to every part of my life.

I was born and raised in an Orthodox Jewish community.

I have 4 siblings (I'm in the middle) and a mom and a dad.

I went to a religious Jewish school called Yeshivah, where we studied ancient Hebrew and learned how to pray in Hebrew too.

I also did ordinary things
that most other kids do like...

- Read books.

- Go to summer camp.

- Eat lots of ice cream.

- And I loved watching baseball—go, Yankees!

One of the mitzvahs we practice is **Shabbos** שַׁבָּת (Shahb-bos), also called Shabbat.

Shabbos happens every week for 24 hours.

Yes, every single week.

It begins Friday night at sundown and lasts until Saturday night at nightfall.

Jewish people believe that Shabbos is a day of rest because when God created the world, he rested on the 7th day.

So, for us, that means...

- no work for grownups,

- no iPads or screen time for kids,

- no cooking, cleaning, or electrical devices for anyone,

- and definitely no homework—yay!

What happens on Shabbos?

Families come together to share a special meal.

You get to be with all the people you love most without any distractions.

There is prayer, singing, games, conversation, and lots of joy.

(It's kind of like having Thanksgiving every weekend!)

Many parts of my life as an observant Jewish person might sound different or new to you.

**Like, did you know
I only eat kosher food?**

Kosher literally means "genuine or proper."

So, eating kosher means I only eat certain foods in specific ways.

Some of the foods I do not eat are pork, bacon, crab, lobster, or other seafood.

There are some foods I can eat, but just not in combination.

Like, I don't eat any meat with milk.

(That's a fancy way of saying no cheeseburgers.)

But don't feel sad for me! Almost anywhere you find Jewish people, you can find great kosher food to eat.

Just look for the kosher labels on food packaging!

You might be asking yourself,

Why do Jewish people eat kosher food and celebrate Shabbos?

Because we believe this is what God wants us to do, and that's really important to us.

Jewish people have been carefully keeping these traditions for thousands of years and passing them down from grownups to kids for generations.

Throughout history, Jewish people have sometimes had to quit jobs or lose customers in order to respect our religious laws, like closing our stores or businesses every Shabbos.

We do it because our parents and ancestors did it before us.

It's a way of keeping our traditions alive.

They are
a part of
who we are.

And there are so many other practices that are a part of my everyday life and Jewish identity.

I pray 3 times a day—in the morning, in the afternoon, and at night.

I wear a **kippah** כיפה (kip-pah) or **yarmulke** (YAH-mi-koh) on my head every day.

I learn Torah whenever I can.

And there are holidays to celebrate, like

Passover פֶּסַח,

Hannakuh חֲנֻכָּה (Chaa-nuh-ka),

Rosh Hashanah רֹאשׁ הַשָּׁנָה (Row-shh Ha-sha-na),

Yom Kippur יוֹם כִּפּוּר (Yom Kip-pur),

and Purim פּוּרִים (Poo-reem).

Some of these holidays are really fun and you get great gifts **(like on Hanukkah)**, and on others you get to dress up, wear costumes, and give out lots of candy **(like Purim)**!

Some of these holidays include the Jewish New Year **(Rosh Hashanah)** and the holiest day of the year where we pray and fast **(Yom Kippur)**.

We celebrate when young people turn 12 or 13 with a huge party, dancing, and reading from the Torah, to symbolize growing up and becoming responsible for keeping God's commandments.

Remember when I told you there was too much about Judaism to fit in 1 book?

This is what I mean!

So, who are the

They are the descendants o

Jewish People?

Abraham, Isaac, and Jacob.

Long ago, Jewish people were enslaved in Egypt for many years.

God eventually freed them and took them out of Egypt.

And God gave the Torah to Moses and the Jewish people on Mt. Sinai.

Thousands of years ago, Jews lived in their ancestral home of Israel, where the temple stood in Jerusalem.

Today, 1 wall of that holy temple still stands—I was lucky enough to visit once!

Because of the long history of Judaism, Jews can be found almost anywhere and everywhere.

In fact, there are about 14 million Jews around the world.*

*If you're curious whether you're Jewish, look to your mother's side of the family! Judaism is a matrilineal religion, so follow the ancestry of your mother to find out if that's a part of your story too!

Throughout history, Jewish people have been persecuted* just for being Jewish.

So, they have had to move to many new places to find a peaceful and better life.

*Persecuted means discriminated against, hated, and treated unfairly.

That means you can find Jewish people in almost every size, shape, color, or country.

You can find different Jewish cuisine, cultures, and even languages based on where they come from.

According to the Torah, all people were created in God's image.

Which means that all people have inherent goodness and deserve to be treated with respect and kindness.

The Jewish people believe that the values of being kind, respecting our parents and our elders, giving to charities, helping others, and loving your neighbor are all essential to Judaism.

This is called Chessed חֶסֶד,
(Che-sed).

Chessed is all about doing good deeds and helping others.

Which is what I strive to do every day.

Judaism is about living for a higher purpose and bringing joy and a sense of mission to our lives.

I'm not perfect and don't always get it right, but I'm trying.

And I'm thankful to my many friends, family, community, rabbis, and God, who help me on this journey.

Outro

Now that you know what Judaism is and the different ways to celebrate it, there are many ways to continue educating yourself about Judaism and learn more about Jewish people.

Grownups, this is the time to share your experiences with either being Jewish or those around you who are Jewish, and what this religion means and how it has impacted you.

This is also a good time to teach kids about religious persecution, baseless hatred, and how it has impacted lots of religions worldwide. By learning about religions and groups other than our own, we discover the beauty and similarities between us that we never knew existed, which create a more meaningful, equal, and diverse world.

About The Author

M. M. Friedman (he/him) wrote this book for any kid or parent out there discovering or wanting to discover their Jewish heritage. Growing up Jewish and religious in faith, he wanted to display the beauty, depth, and possible fun of one of the world's most famous but minuscule religions.

M. M. Friedman has visited many countries and traveled the world to see how different Jewish cultures live, pray, and interact with one another, trying new foods and experiencing new customs along the way.

This book is meant to be a beginner's guide to Judaism for both grownups and kids, describing some of the practices and holidays Jewish people honor, as well as offering outsiders a newfound understanding and, ultimately, appreciation of the Jewish people.

Discover more at akidsco.com

www.ingramcontent.com/pod-product-compliance
Lightning Source LLC
Chambersburg PA
CBHW061359010526
44107CB00012B/988